The Only Place For Me

An Ulsterman's Verse

D1495120

The Only Place For Me

An Ulsterman's Verse
by
Bill Nesbitt

illustrated by Rowel Friers ✳

The
Blackstaff
Press

British Library Cataloguing in Publication Data

Nesbitt, Bill
  The only place for me.
  I. Title
  821' 914   PR6064.E

  ISBN 0-85640-268-0

© Introduction by Walter Love, 1982
© Poems by Bill Nesbitt, 1982

Published by Blackstaff Press Limited
3 Galway Park, Dundonald, BT16 0AN

All rights reserved

Printed in Northern Ireland by
Universities Press Limited

Contents

Introduction

From time to time listeners to the 'Day by Day' programme on BBC Radio Ulster drop me a line enclosing something which they think may be of interest to other listeners. A few months ago one lady sent us a poem about Belfast called 'The only place for me'. She didn't know who had written it, and when Louis Gilbert subsequently read it out we didn't realise what the result would be. Within minutes the phone calls started, and for several weeks letters flooded in asking for copies. And it didn't take long to find out who the author was. Bill Nesbitt, already a familiar voice to 'Day by Day' listeners, confirmed that it was something which he had written some time ago.

In fact, the version which Louis had read had a number of extra verses added, but Bill himself read the original version for us. Because of the enormous response to the poem we decided to run a poetry competition borrowing the words of Bill's title. And again the response was most encouraging, and we were quick to realise just how many people there are from all walks of life who feel a strong urge to write with affection of places dear to their hearts. Altogether, more than 800 copies of the original poem were sent out to those who requested them, and the competition subsequently produced an entry of more than 200. It was felt appropriate to invite both Bill and Louis to judge those entries – which wasn't an easy job, because the general standard was extremely high.

A recurring theme in many of the poems was the desire to look back, sometimes with a tinge of sadness, to places the writers knew as children; places which have often changed out of all recognition, and which can never be replaced. Bill Nesbitt has these feelings very strongly. But more than that, he has the happy knack of seeing and registering in his mind's eye a host of things which others often take for granted, or have forgotten all about, and of capturing these memories and recording them through the words he writes.

Some of the memories are personal to me too, like the thrills of a very young traveller on the Bangor train. To the best of my knowledge the Bangor train doesn't pass through a strange place called Ballymagheroo. Which might well be a pity because there are some wonderful Ulster characters who live there, and some quite extraordinary events happen there from time to time. . . Sometimes the subjects are comparatively trivial, like the crisp tale of 'The wee blue beg', or the crisis of a broken television set. But whatever the subject, Bill writes with the greatest of affection of the land he loves. As he says in 'Dear Ulster',

> Dear Ulster, fairest of the fair,
> But a paradox, that's true –
> In all the whole wide world, I swear
> There's nowhere quite like you!

There's only one point on which I'd dare to disagree with Bill and what he writes. And that's when he says, 'I'm just an oul' cod of a rhymer. . .' I rather suspect that, like me, you too will find great enjoyment from the pages of this book. And may he keep on writing, and reading his poetry to us for many years to come.

Walter Love

Prologue

I'm just an oul' cod of a rhymer,
    no Wordsworth or Browning am I –
If you say that my verses aren't 'poems',
    that's something I will not deny;
The words that I write aren't immortal,
    and won't bring me fortune or fame,
But so long as there's folk who enjoy them,
    who cares if they know not my name!

For I love writing rhymes of my country,
    of the people and places I know,
Of the fields and the rivers of Ulster,
    in the sun and the rain and the snow,
Of the noise and the grime of the city,
    the gossip in some country town –
Sure, as long as my pen can describe them,
    who cares if they bring no renown?

I'll write of the crack of the townie,
    I'll write of the farmer as well;
I'll write of our ways, our traditions,
    I'll put down the stories they tell;
I'll scribble my verse as I travel,
    and struggle to make my tales rhyme –
With my pen and my wee bits of paper,
    sure, I'm having a wonderful time!

In a main street, or wee country loaney,
    there's always a verse to be found;
There's a tale for the ears that will hear it,
    there's a story in each single sound;
In front of the range in a cottage,
    by the fireside in some council flat –
There's many's a yarn to be gathered
    as down at the table you're sat. . .

To write of the people, the things that I love,
    is really not much of a task,
For Ulster's just full of wee stories,
    and to hear them you just have to ask –
The old man, whose life's reached its twilight,
    the wee lad who's just starting out;
The tinker, the tailor, the soldier, the sailor –
    there's lots to be writing about!

A fisherman down by the river,
    the thrill of a salmon that's leaping;
The chorus of birds in the morning,
    the stillness when Nature is sleeping;
The rattle of churns in a farmyard,
    the sight of a young lover's tears –
It's Nature herself guides my pencil
    whenever a new verse appears!

Yes, it's easy to write about Ulster,
    the richness, the warmth of her heart,
So, even if I am no Wordsworth,
    and my verses aren't reckoned as Art,
Well, so long as you like them, I'm happy,
    and I will continue to try
To write my wee verses – not poems!
    Just a cod of an oul' rhyming guy. . .

The only place for me

I'll speak to you of Belfast, stranger, if you want to know,
So listen, and I'll tell you why I love this city so. . .

BELFAST. . . is an Ulsterman, with features dour and grim,
It's a pint of creamy porter, a Sunday morning hymn,
A steaming pasty supper, or vinegar with peas,
A little grimy café where they'll serve you 'farmhouse' teas,
A banner on July the Twelfth, a sticky toffee apple,
An ancient little Gospel Hall, a Roman Catholic chapel,
A *Telly* boy with dirty face, a slice of apple tart,
A fry upon a Saturday, hot 'coal-breek' on a cart,
A Corporation gas-man, complete with bowler hat,
A wee shop on a corner with a friendly bit of chat,
An oul' lad in a duncher, a woman in a shawl,
A pinch of snuff, a tatie farl, a loyal Orange Hall,
A tobacco smell in York Street, a bag of 'yella man',
An Easter egg that's dyed in whin, a slice of Ormo pan,
A youngster with some sprickly-begs inside a wee jam-jar,
A meeting at the Custom House, an old Victorian bar,
Mud-banks on the Lagan when the tide is running low,
A man collecting 'refuse', bonfires in Sandy Row,
A bag of salty dullis, a bowl of Irish stew,
And goldfish down in Gresham Street, a preacher at a queue,
A portrait of King Billy upon a gable wall,
A flower-seller on a stool outside the City Hall,
A half-moon round a doorstep, a 'polisman' on guard,
A pedlar crying 'Delph for Regs!', a little whitewashed yard. . .

And there's your answer, stranger, and now I'm sure you'll see
Why Belfast is the only place in all the world for me.

The Ulsterman

Living in a thousand places, Mississippi to the Bann,
Man of many different faces – calls himself an Ulsterman. . .

Under shadow of the gantry, dwarfed by heaven-hugging cranes,
Waiting for the finish whistle, blessed rest from labour's pains.

Transport home, by kind permission of the Belfast Corporation,
Conductor's cheery Ulster accent defying all interpretation.

Home to tea of fish and chips, freshly-buttered soda bread,
Wages lying on the table, week of working duly paid.

Shaving with a week-old blade – always shaves on Friday night –
Scraping over granite face; epitome of Ulster's might!

Standing there outside the bookie's (seems as if he's always done),
Full of equine erudition – what way will the favourite run?

Creamy pint of porter adding wit to conversation;
Memorable decisions on the running of the nation.

Brother living in the country, Tobergill or Tandragee,
Sowing barley, tending cattle, no one half so good as he.

Standing at the local crossroad, waiting there for Willie John;
Words of wisdom, words of greeting – bit of dealing going on.

State of crops, and price of beasts, cocking up a weather eye,
Tomorrow's labours all dependent on the colour of the sky.

Family there for generations, daylight come and daylight gone,
Opinions and beliefs unchanging, while the world goes marching on.

Cousin living out abroad, doing well with all he owns;
Hasn't lost his Ulster accent (mid-Atlantic overtones!);

2

Doing work he'd never dreamed of, trying things he'd never dare,
Sometimes thinking of his homeland, pride of heritage still there.

Wonder what it looks like now, in my birthplace by the sea?
Wonder if they still remember – do they ever think of me?

Really must go back some day, had enough of foreign lands –
Like to see the lads out marching, hear again the noisy bands.

Not a bad old life I'm living, money good, people fine;
Have to stay here – can't help missing all the things that once were
    mine.

Living in a thousand places, Mississippi to the Bann,
Man of many different faces – proud to be an Ulsterman. . .

The dale

Now, they've got a reputation in Ballymena town
For savin' every ha'penny, every tanner and half-crown,
But they're very dacent people, respectable, and clean,
And I don't believe a word of it when people call them mean.

But there's one man in particular, whose name I'm keepin' quiet,
Who's the meanest man in Ulster, and no one can deny it;
Beside his stingy manners, oul' Scrooge's deeds would pale,
And I'm sure that you will all agree when you have heard my tale. . .

He'd work his farm the live-long day, he'd rise up at the dawn
And keep on workin' through the dark, long past daylight-gone;
His eldest son was thirty-six, his youngest twenty-three,
And he kept the poor lads at it till they looked as old as he.

Well, he had a great ambition that he wanted to expand
And he had his greedy eye upon his neighbour's bit of land,
Until, one day, to his delight, that land came up for sale –
If he'd have been a spaniel, he'd have gone and wagged his tail!

So he went and saw the daler, and he haggled at the price,
And fought for every shillin' he could possibly entice –
And, after hours of wranglin', the daler made the sale;
I'd swear, he wasn't happy at his profit on the dale!

The signin'-up was organised for nine o'clock next day,
And on the dot, your man arrived; says he, 'How much to pay?'
'Sixty-thousand, eighty-nine', replied the auctioneer,
'That's the price that we agreed. . .' Says he, 'I've got it here. . .'

His eldest son walked in the dure, a bucket in each hand,
Each one overflowin' with the coinage of the land;
Pounds and fivers, fifty-pences, stuffed up to the brim;
Buckets full of money, spillin' at the rim. . .

He threw it on the counter for the office clerk to count,
And it took the poor lad ages, 'twas such a large amount.
But when at last he'd finished, his face was sad to see;
Says he, 'I'm awful sorry – but you're short of twenty pee. . .'

The oul' boy turned round to his son, and gave him fierce abuse;
Says he, 'Ye're just an eejit, and not a pick of use!
'I said to fetch the money – but when ye went and tuk it
'Ye acted like a gommerel. . . for you fetched me
      THE WRONG BUCKET!'

The tick man

Wud ye like a pair of stockin's, missus? A new electric fire?
Some nice elastic thingummies to hide yer oul' spare tyre?
A set o' woolly blankets? Just tell us what ye seek –
I'll give ye anythin' ye want, for a couple o' bob a week. . .

Hello, there, Mrs Watson, and how are you the day?
What's that ye say? Ach, that's a shame – ye haven't got yer pay;
Well, niver mind, I'll tell ye what, next week ye'll pay double?
Aye, that's all right; sure, I don't mind, it isn't any trouble.

Good evenin', Mrs Mooney – I thought ye'd like till know
Thon wee account ye have with me has jist a week till go;
Perhaps there's somethin' else ye'd like? I've got it – jist the job!
Ye can have a leather 'puffy', for another couple o' bob. . .

How's the daughter, Mrs B.? The married one – wee Nell?
D'ye think that maybe she would like a wee account as well?
Now that she's expectin', there's things she must be needin' –
A fine wee girl, thon Nellie; a credit till your breedin'!

Hey, Mrs Mac – I know ye're there! Ye needn't try till hide!
I see ye through the letterbox, standin' there inside!
Ye only owe me fifty bob – c'mon, I won't be hard. . .
(Ach, here, she's diddled me again, she's sneaked out through the
	yard.)

It's a hard oul' job, I must admit, at times it gits me down,
Collectin' all the shillin's as I go upon me roun',
An' I'll niver make me fortune, but still, y'know, it's true
That I've a hundred times more friends than any one of you!

For I have got a secret – I own a magic key
That opens up a storehouse full of treasure; for, y'see,
I can grant your ivery single wish – and you can be unique
And live jist like a millionaire. . . for a couple o' bob a week!

The taxi

I met a girl at the village hop, she said her name was Nancy;
She really was a smasher, and to her I took a fancy;
I asked her could I take her home, she said that she was willin',
But I had to get a taxi, and it cost me thirty shillin'. . .

Now, that's a lot of money, so I asked her for the half,
And, boys, but she was stingy, for she turned, and just walked aff;
I had to pay it all meself – it simply wasnae fair,
And surely it was only right that she should pay her share?

Women! Ach, they're all the same, as selfish as can be,
Preyin' on poor eejits, the likes of you and me;
They'd take your last make, so they would, given half the chance –
And take the sting away from it by callin' it 'romance'.

Well, anyway, this Nancy had gone off and left me stranded;
You must admit, her actions were mighty heavy-handed,
For that thirty bob was all I had, and, och, it made me sick
When the rotten taxi-driver wouldnae take me home on tick. . .

And then the rain came peltin' down, a terrible oul' night,
And I got soaked from head to foot, I must have been a sight.
I walked, and tried to thumb a lift, but nobody would stop;
I tell you, I was scunnered at that stupid village hop!

A good three hours it took me, till I was home in bed,
And, och, the thoughts of vengeance that went runnin' through my
        head!
But, in spite of all the walkin', I found it hard to sleep –
When I thought about that thirty bob, I felt that I could weep!

Well, I saw her at the village hop, time and time again –
A right flirtatious creature, that was brave and plain,
For every week she'd flash her eyes at Tom, or Dick, or Maxie,
And one of them would take her home. . . and always in a taxi!

Well, I let a wheen of months go by, and then I chanced me arm,
And asked to take her home again, with every ounce of charm;
I acted like the memory of that night was far behind me,
And as far as Nancy was concerned, she really couldn't mind me. . .

Well, we went home in a taxi, for that was Nancy's style,
And it cost me thirty bob again, but I paid up with a smile,
For I'd found that Nancy's father was the man who did the drivin' –
Because of her, his business was absolutely thrivin'!

So I set me cap at Nancy, and her and me got wed –
I'd always sworn to wed a lass who'd got a business head!
And now we've got three daughters, they're beautiful, and sweet,
And I don't own a taxi. . . I own a bloomin' fleet!

The vote-catcher

I'm goin' into politics, and I'm sure I'll get your backin',
For I'm the man the country needs when leadership is lackin',
And when I'm made dictator, you'll all sit up and grin –
So vote for me – I promise you'll be glad you put me in!

I've talked with politicians who're already in the game
I asked one man for his advice (I'm sure you'd know his name!);
He told me that my policies he wouldn't trust a bit –
When I mentioned all the things I'd planned, he nearly had a fit!

I'll cut the price of yella man to a ha'penny a lump,
And slap a tax on Lambeg drums of two pee for a thump;
I'll declare a public holiday every time it's sunny,
And make an eight-hour workin' week – and double all your money.

I'll give you lots of benefits, without insurance stamps;
I'll offer you free holidays in Billy Butlin's camps;
Fags at ten for fifteen pee, with a Guinness thrown in –
And every time you do the pools, I'll guarantee you'll win!

If you didn't feel like workin', you could go to the Buroo –
They'd treat you with civility, and you wouldn't have to queue;
I'll fit out Corporation Street with carpets wall to wall,
And give you dinner on the house each time you made a call!

I'll give you all big motor-cars, and tailored Burton suits,
And Shankill Road musicians will get gold-plated flutes;
For video recorders, you'll have fifty years to pay,
And, legally, I'll let you throw your unpaid bills away!

No doubt about it, I'm your man, on that you must agree,
So when election day arrives, please vote, vote, vote for me;
Like the other politicians, I'm goin' to see it through –
For, if they can make false promises, then I can do it, too!

Night watch

The kettle's on the brazier, an' while the water's hatin'
I'm lookin' at the cinders dyin' slowly in the gratin',
An' it seems to me that I can see, within each glowin' ember
The faces that I used to know, the old friends I remember. . .

There's William John, the blacksmith's son, with catapult an' all,
An' Sammy Smith, still practisin' with thon oul' cricket ball,
An' there's wee Mickey Murtagh, the lad that did the mitchin' –
An' there's wee Jane, my first sweetheart, her freckles still
   bewitchin'. . .

I see the mate I used to have when I first started workin',
With his duncher, an' his dungarees, his greasy leather jerkin,
An' the boss who terrified me, when a trade I started learnin';
Ach, he wasn't such a bad oul' stick, in spite of all his girnin'. . .

Look – there's the Reverend Thingummy, seekin' my salvation,
Still givin' me a taste or two of hellfire an' damnation;
I even see my first wee dog – I mind his name was Rex –
An' there's the Head I had at school, with his big thick horn-rimmed
   specs. . .

But, suddenly, the cinders shift, the figures disappear,
Another face is formin' there, a face I hold so dear. . .
The only one I've ever loved, the lass I made my wife;
Och, since she passed away, it's been an awful lonely life. . .

Ah well, the kettle's boilin', it's time I brewed the tay;
It's no good sittin' here just dreamin' half the night away.
My bones are far too ould for this, I'll very soon retire
An' say goodbye to all my friends in this wee cinder fire. . .

Breakdown

My eyes are shot, my hair is grey, my wits are at an end;
I'm driven to distraction, I'm goin' round the bend,
I'll tell you, lads, I'm crackin' up, on that you can depend. . .
Ach, can't you see I'm slowly goin' crazy?
I'm all tensed up – you see the way my poor oul' hands are shakin'?
I'm all a-tremble, head to foot, my very knees are quakin',
And I'm rattlin' with the tranquilisers that I have gone and taken,
For nowadays my life is far from aisy. . .

The missus, she's as bad as me, she's nearly at 'high doh';
The two of us are up the walls (as if you didn't know!);
We're gettin' on each other's backs, we're due to have a blow,
And we haven't passed a civil word all night. . .
Since half-past-six, or thereabouts, I've gone through thirty fegs;
I've nearly worn the carpet out, never mind my legs;
I can hardly see the room at all, me eyes have got such begs –
I'm in a fierce predicament, all right!

Me nerves are tight as fiddle-strings, me temper's none too sweet;
Oul' Nick himself would have a job my rotten twist to beat –
I'm sure I'm the contrariest oul' fellow in the street – ·
I'm really just not at myself at all. . .
When you see the way I'm actin' up, you'll swear there's somethin'
       lackin',
But you needn't try to talk to me, for I've no time for crackin';
And if you try to cheer me up, I'm sure to send you packin',
And as sure as eggs, I'm headed for a fall. . .

I'm thrawn as sin, without a doubt, and that's just not like me;
I'm not the aisy-goin' sort of man I used to be;
It's not my nature, so it's not, I'm sure you must agree,
For I used to love me little bit of jokin'. . .
But the raison for me present form, I'm sure you'll understand
Whenever I explain to you why things are none too grand –
No wonder I'm distracted; it's enough to bate the band,
You see. . . my television set is broken!!!

The antique

They have a little antique shop in Ballymagheroo;
Its owner is a dear old girl called Millicent Mulgrew,
And I've no wish to be unkind, but, really, truth to tell,
Milly's near as ould herself as anythin' she'll sell!

Her shop is filled with curios, all sorts of bric-a-brac,
And boys, as far as sellin' goes, she really has the knack!
A rusting relic of the past, the bones of some oul' king –
Our Milly had her head screwed on; she'd sell you anything!

One day, a Yankee tourist passed through Ballymagheroo,
And he collected antiques, like all Yankees seem to do. . .
In the middle of the window, an axe had pride of place,
And it brought a look of pleasure to that Yankee tourist's face.

The label on the hatchet said, 'The Bargain of the Week –
An ancient axe we guarantee as really most unique;
An object for the connoisseur to place upon his shelf –
The weapon used by no one else but Finn M'Cool himself!'

The tourist hurried on inside; said he, 'Ma'am, name your price –
I fancy that old hatchet, it's really very nice!'
Says Milly, 'I won't rob you, for I like to think I'm fair,
So I'll ask five thousand dollars. . . and, after all, it's rare.'

'You've got a deal – I'll pay it!' cried the tourist in delight,
'The axe of Finn M'Cool himself – a real fantastic sight!
It's the bargain of a lifetime – but I'll make a wee admission;
I'd love to know the reason for its well-preserved condition. . .'

'Why shouldn't it be well-preserved?' says Millicent Mulgrew,
'Sure, Finn M'Cool's oul' hatchet is just as good as new!
It's been looked after through the years by men who knew their
        crafts –
Why, eighteen blades have been replaced . . . and twenty-seven
        shafts!'

13

The burglars

At the dawn of the day, the mists lay grey
    on Ballymagheroo,
With folk asleep in slumber deep. . .
    except for a certain two,
For Big Black Dan and Cross-Eyed Stan
    were criminally bent;
While people slept, round the houses crept
    with nefarious intent. . .

Not a creature stirred, not a sound was heard
    as they planned their dirty deed —
They were after the cash of the Widow Nash,
    and their hearts were filled with greed,
For she had around three thousand pound,
    but never spent two dee,
And the boyos thought that she really ought
    to share it with them, you see!

As still as a mouse, round the back of the house
    the ruffians slid with stealth,
And they shinned the drain to the window pane
    of the room where she hid her wealth;
In a couple of ticks, with their criminal tricks
    they'd opened the window wide —
A skelly around — not a sight nor a sound —
    in a flash they were safe inside. . .

Not a single squeak, not a floorboard's creak
    as they tiptoed across the room;
It was still as death, and they held their breath
    as they tried to pierce the gloom;
They crossed the floor, then they saw the door
    of the safe that held the cash,
And their hearts stood still as they used their skill
    to open it, in a flash. . .

With lumps in their throats, they stuffed the notes
    into a waiting sack,
Then off they went, in great content,
    leaving no trace nor track –
Rich! Rich! Rich!
                 Over field and ditch
    they flew, as if on air. . .
But they weren't so cute – when they checked their loot,
    their hearts knew black despair!

It wasn't so funny, for all that money
    (thousands of pounds, that's true!)
Wasn't worth two dee, because, you see,
    the pair of them hadn't a clue
That the Widow Nash was so fond of cash
    that she never went near the bank,
And the lads had forgot the one weak spot –
    that the Widow Nash was a crank. . .

The lady was saft – completely daft –
    and she'd really have been surprised
If she'd been told that the country's gold
    had now been decimalised!
And Big Black Dan and Cross-Eyed Stan
    wouldn't buy fur coats –
Nor even suits – for their hard-earned loot
    was all in ten-bob notes!

The well-wisher

Hello – how are ye, Martha? Ye're lukkin' quare an' well,
Though they say ye haven't been yerself, at laste, so I heard tell;
Were ye under the doctor, tell us? What did he have to say?
He must have done ye a power of good, for ye're lukkin' grand
    the day!

Of coorse, that's apart from the one thing – yer cheeks are a wee
    bit paled,
But sure, if ye haven't been too good, it's natural that ye've failed –
D'ye know, I was tould ye were very bad, an' knockin' at death's
    dure
But ye'd never think it to see ye – ye're thrivin', that's for sure!

I'd say ye've lost a stone or two, but ye couldn't be bad to that,
For Martha, ye must admit it, ye were always a wee bit fat!
I'd never have known ye, that's a fact, ye look so wee, and nate,
But, sure, it suits ye, Martha, and ye're lukkin' quare an' great!

Ye're a wee bit shaky on yer feet, but, Martha, would ye care?
Nobody'd know that ye've been sick, ye luk so well, I swear!
But still an' all, take my advice, and ease off for a bit –
Although, mind you, for all that, ye're lukkin' brave an' fit!

Ye really do luk good, ye know, for bein' through the mill,
Although, of coorse, ye're bound till have the marks upon ye still,
But, Martha, here, I've seen folk worse, afore they went an' died –
But you? Ye're lukkin' smashin'. . . if ye put yer face aside. . .

Ach, Martha, dear, don't get me wrong – yer face is not too bad;
It's just a wee bit thinner, but, sure, ye should be glad,
For after all, let's face it, ye're not no Dairy Queen. . .
Though ye look a fair bit better than ever I have seen. . .

What's that? Ach, here, ye've tuk the huff – I wasn't bein' rude!
Here, Martha, won't ye listen? It's just for your own good. . .
Well, now, wud ye believe it – she's went an' gone away. . .
There's just no pleasin' some folk – whatever did I say?

The genie

I got into a row with the missus,
    I was in a terrible state,
For when weemin are warrin', they're fiercesome,
    and leave ye not feelin' too great;
I was right, but sure that didn't matter,
    for with weemin ye just cannot win –
So I walked out of the house in a temper;
    if I'd stayed, I'd have done the wife in!

I made a beeline for me local,
    like an arrow that's straight from the bow,
For a pint and a wee bit of quiet,
    and to get me head showered, y'know;
'What's the matter?' sez Johnny the barman,
    'Did ye get out the wrong side o' the bed?'
'Ach, the wife's at her naggin',' I answered;
    Sez Johnny, 'Houl' on – enough said!'

Then he set a grand pint on the counter,
    and it tasted like nectar, I swear –
Then another I had, and another,
    just to help me my burdens to bear,
And then I'd a couple o' wee ones,
    and soon I began to feel grand –
Sez Johnny, 'Here, Willie – go aisy!
    Ye'll soon not be able to stand!'

'Ach, Johnny, ye're worse than the missus
    – ye're soundin' just like her yerself!
'And now be so kind as to hand me
    thon bottle that's up on the shelf.
'I can't say I know just what's in it,
    but I'm willin' to give it a try,
'For the shape of it's sort of intriguin'
    – whatever the price is, I'll buy!'

Well, he handed it down – it was ancient!
   Covered with cobwebs and dusty,
With queer foreign writin' upon it,
   and a smell that was terrible musty,
And the cork was near crumbled to pieces;
   pullin' it out was no joke,
But I managed – then, all of a sudden,
   out poured a great column of smoke!

And the smoke took the shape of a figure,
   and a great boomin' voice echoed loud:
'I'm your genie, oh Master! Whatever your wish,
   I promise I'll do ye real proud!
'Silver and gold, untold riches
   to keep ye the rest of yer life –'
Sez I, 'Here, ye're terrible dacent;
   perhaps ye could sort out the wife?'

'Consider it done, little Master!
   Whenever you go home the night,
'Ye'll find that yer missus is different,
   ye'll be clappin' yer hands in delight!
'A beautiful blonde, and obedient,
   who'll always agree you're the boss,
'Who'll do all she can for yer comfort,
   and furthermore, never get cross!'

But then, the disaster, it happened,
   an occurrence I'll never forget,
For a stupid wee drunk in the corner
   soon had us all soakin' wet –
He'd spotted the smoke, the wee eejit,
   and kicked up a terrible fuss,
Pulled the fire-hose from its cradle,
   and aimed the contraption at us!

Well, that was the end of the genie;
   the column of smoke just a puff
Lickin' the neck of the bottle
   – the genie'd gone off in the huff!

18

So I turned on the drunk in a fury,
    and let out a terrible roar –
But me elbow, it nudged the oul' bottle,
    and smashed it to bits on the floor. . .

Ach, the missus is not a hate different,
    her tongue's still as sharp as a knife,
And we argue the toss day and daily
    – thon wumman's the bane of me life!
And night after night, I'm out early,
    huntin' each bar in the city
For a bottle that might hold a genie
    – but not much luck yet, more's the pity!

The living saint

I know that you're a dacent lad –
You've tould me brave and often –
And, when other folk are troubled bad,
Your heart's the first to soften;
The epitome of all that's good,
And expert at the prayin',
You always do the things you should –
Or so you keep on sayin'. . .

A lover of your fellow man,
As selfless as can be,
Helping others when you can
(Or so you've said to me);
When people find that they're in need
They'll always turn to you;
You'll never let them down – indeed,
You've told me, so it's true. . .

20

When poor men find their larders bare
And nothing on the shelf,
You give them what you have to spare –
You told me so, yourself.
You never think an evil thought
Or do what isn't right,
But act exactly as you ought –
You said that, just last night. . .

Other people have their woes
And share of fear and friction,
But you are not the same as those
Who haven't your conviction.
You really are an upright man,
A Godly virtuoso –
And you make certain, when you can,
That everybody knows so. . .

You preach at everyone you meet
To be as good as you are,
But of all the people in the street,
Very, very few are.
I know that you're a living saint
And well, well worth the meetin',
While a saint is something that I ain't –
For so you keep repeatin'. . .

Your many virtues you've extolled
When you have had a minute;
Your goodly deeds you've often told,
So there must be something in it. . .
You share your money, drink and grub –
I've got no cause to doubt it. . .
But I only wish you'd shut your gub
And brag no more about it!

The purple spotted thing

Old Uncle Fred, he died in bed the other Friday night,
But he didn't suffer in the least, for as usual, he was tight.
The lawyer came to read the will, our eyes were sad and wet,
As we held our breaths, and waited to see what we would get. . .

Aunt Dot, she got the house, of course; his daughters got the cash;
To Uncle Joe, he left his flute, and favourite Orange sash.
But me? I got a parcel, with sealing-wax and string,
And when I opened it, I saw . . . a purple spotted *thing!*

Now, purple spotted things are fine, if you're the type that's keen,
But that was just the ugliest that I have ever seen!
I tell you, boys, it made me sick, it really was a shocker,
And just the very look of it near put me off my rocker!

I went to bed, but couldn't sleep – each time I closed my eyes
I dreamed of that darned spotted thing – but twenty times the size. . .
So when I rose next morning, I dumped it in the bin,
But the binman took one look at it, and thumped me on the chin. . .

Well, then I had a great idea; I tied it up with string,
And took it to a dealer who buys most anything,
And I must admit that dealer was very, very nice –
He took it off my hands, and gave a fairly decent price.

Now, that was that; I rubbed my hands, and trotted home with glee,
Happy at the distance between that darned thing and me.
It chanced to be my birthday, so I went and had a fling
With the money that I'd got for it, that purple spotted thing.

Such a night I had that night – I really went to town,
But when I woke next morning, I found I'd cause to frown,
For I heard a knock upon the door (my head split at the racket) –
'Good morning!' said the postman, and handed me a packet. . .

Well, I put it on the table, and quickly opened it,
And when I saw what it contained, I nearly had a fit!
On a card inside was written, 'Happy Birthday, from Aunt Dot –
I bought this from a dealer, to match the one you've got!'

I'm driven to distraction, my head is near astray,
And I'd give you everything I have to take that thing away!
If Uncle Fred was not so dead, for him I'd gladly swing –
For life is not worth living . . . with a purple spotted thing!

The lost flute

I'm driven half demented, I don't know what to do;
I've hunted for it everywhere – I'm in an awful stew,
For I'm sort of lost without it, it really was a beaut. . .
So, please, please, won't you tell me – have you seen my wee tin flute?

I've looked in all the bedrooms, and in the bathroom, too,
And underneath the jaw-box, but I couldn't find a clue;
I've rummaged in the sideboard, I've hunted every place –
Whatever am I goin' to do? It's vanished without trace!

I'll never find another with a tone so clear and sweet,
And to hear me playin' thon wee flute would give your ears a treat;
A loyal song, a rebel tune, a real oul' Irish air –
It made no different what it played, thon wee flute didn't care.

My granda bought it for me, when I was just turned ten,
But that's a wheen of years ago, and I've grown ould since then,
And the years have turned me kind of sour, my skin is dry, and
    yellowed,
But the notes from thon wee flute of mine, the passing years have
    mellowed.

23

It's not the sort of instrument you'd call sophisticated;
In the eyes of all the highbrows, it's very lowly rated,
And yet, y'know, I'd much prefer to have my wee tin flute
Than a concert grand piano, Stradivarius, or lute.

Thon flute and me together, we've been through thick and thin,
And helped to make folk happy, no matter where we've bin;
We've played at wakes and weddin's, in sorrow and in joy,
From Derry to Dunadry, from Kells to Clandeboye.

Och, I miss it awful badly, without it I feel lost,
And I couldn't buy one like it, no, not at any cost;
I could aisy get another that would surely look the part,
But there's not one made that could replace thon wee flute in my
    heart.

I mind, when I was just sixteen, I joined the local band,
And everyone agreed it was the best in all the land;
We swept the competition boards – and, in all modesty,
I'd say the reason was because of thon wee flute and me!

Well, now it's gone, my heart is broke, I'm very near despair –
I've looked, and looked, and looked but I can't find it anywhere;
There's only one thing left to do – I'll shoot myself at dawn,
For I just can't go on livin', now my wee tin flute is gone!

The gossip

Now, Mrs Murphy, you're like me,
    a dacent, honest crature;
We don't go in for gossipin',
    nor nothin' of that nature –
We're not like some that I could name,
    of that you can be sure,
And we're not scandal-mongers,
    like yer wumman there, nixt dure!

I wouldn't say she's dirty,
    for I'm not unkind, I hope,
But I'll tell you this, her oul' man hides
    his cash beneath the soap,
And I wouldn't say her mouth is big,
    I'm not the sort that jeers,
But every time she speaks, she washes
    right behind her ears. . .

It's not for me to say, of coorse,
    it's no concern of mine,
But I've heard she hits the bottle,
    and drinks the oul' chape wine,
And dear help thon wee man of hers,
    for she wouldn't pay her Maker;
They say he only married her
    'cause no one else would take her. . .

Ach, I'm not one for meddlin',
    but have you ever seen
A wumman half so throughother
    – I've never seen her clean!
The likes of you and me work hard,
    from morn till night we're sloggin',
But she never does a hand's turn,
    and she laves the whole house boggin'. . .

If you knew about her goin's-on,
    your hair would stand on end,
But I don't hould with spreadin' tales,
    on that you can depend;
Yet, still, I'll tell you one thing
    (don't breathe it till a sowl) –
The milkman is her fancy man,
    at laste, so I've heard toul'. . .

Now, you know me, I wouldn't say
    a thing that wasn't true,
And I honestly believe
    in givin' credit where it's due,
But thon wumman, she's the limit,
    she's the lowest of the low;
That's gospel, Mrs Murphy,
    or I wouldn't tell you so. . .

I must admit, I do enjoy
    a bit of cosy crack,
But you'll never catch me talkin'
    behind somebody's back,
So here's a word of sound advice,
    just for your own good –
Your wumman's always spreadin' tales
    around the neighbourhood. . .

The things that I could tell ye
    that I've heard about thon wumman –
But I'll lave them for some other time,
    for luk, now, here's her comin'!
I think that you should go on home,
    for you don't want till mate her,
So bye-bye, Mrs Murphy
    – I'll maybe see you later. . .

Hello, there, Mrs Wilson!
    You're lukkin' quare and fine;
I'm glad till see you, for you've come
    in just the nick of time,

For, ach, thon Murphy wumman
   has driven me astray –
Here, listen till I tell you. . .
   though it's not for me till say. . .

A farmer's day

I went out till the tractor this mornin',
    she was terrible awkward tae start,
And then I discovered the raison,
    for I spotted a very loose part,
So I looked for a spanner tae fix it,
    but divil the spanner I found,
But, while I was lookin', I noticed
    a brave taste of water around. . .

Then I found that the cow-trough was leakin',
    and I thought that I'd put on a patch. . .
I went up tae the house for the solder
    ('twas just half-past-six by me watch),
But, by seven, I still hadnae found it –
    tae get on with the job I was itchin' –
And then, tae me horror, I spotted
    a hen runnin' loose in the kitchen. . .

So I went tae the hen-run, disgusted,
    tae look for the break in the wire,
But then, as I went, I remembered
    a job I'd tae do in the byre;
I hadnae gone halfway the distance
    afore the rain started tae fall,
And I heard the oul' bull start tae gulder;
    he didnae sound happy at all. . .

I decided tae go down an' calm him,
    for thon baste, he was worth a few pound,
And I had tae protect me investment,
    for cash doesnae grow in the ground!
All these footery things were fierce tryin',
    for I cudnae get on with me labour,
Then, would you belave, tae crown matters,
    I chanced tae bump into me neighbour. . .

He cud talk the hind leg aff a donkey –
    and the fore-leg an' all, so he could;

I tried tae escape, but I cudnae,
    for it's not in me way tae be rude,
So he blethered and blethered for ages,
    he cudnae keep quiet at all —
And then, at long last, he remembered
    the raison he'd paid me a call. . .

He toul' me his tractor was broken,
    and he needed tae use it, real bad;
If it wasnae tae be too much bother,
    could he borrow the one that I had?
I toul' him, 'Av coorse'; then I minded
    that I wasnae able tae lend it,
For, what with one thing and another,
    I still hadnae managed tae mend it!

So I went for the spanner tae fix it,
    but divil the spanner I found,
And while I was lookin', I noticed
    a brave taste of water around;
The cow-trough was leakin' — I left it;
    I'd worked hard enough for the day;
'Twas dark now, me labour was finished —
    aye, a farmer works hard for his pay!

Good enough for me

She isn't over handsome, and her tongue is like a knife,
But still and all, I'm fond of her, for Mary Jane's my wife;
She's not the sort would ever pass in high society,
But what's good enough for Mary Jane is good enough for me!

She hasn't got the sort of looks to launch a thousand ships,
And you'd not feel too romantic when she puckers up her lips;
She'd win no beauty contest, on that I must agree,
But what's good enough for Mary Jane is good enough for me!

Her features might be sour at times, and like a Lurgan spade,
And she's got a way of nagging that would cut you like a blade;
There's folk who say I'm henpecked, and sure, I'm bound to be
When what's good enough for Mary Jane is good enough for me!

At thinking, I'm no expert, for I haven't got much brain,
But you couldn't say the same at all for my old Mary Jane –
She's got her wits about her, it's very clear to see,
So what's good enough for Mary Jane is good enough for me!

I must admit, the only time I ever used my head,
Was when I went and faced her, and the two of us got wed;
She's very fond of books, and art, and knows her history,
And what's good enough for Mary Jane is good enough for me!

I wouldn't say she's perfect, for I'm not the sort to brag,
But she turns her nose up at the drink, and wouldn't touch a fag!
There's not a lass in Ulster that's half as good as she,
And what's good enough for Mary Jane is good enough for me!

I never fancied children much, or thought I'd be a da,
But Mary Jane, she changed my mind, and now she is a ma –
We've seven of a family, the youngest only three,
For what's good enough for Mary Jane is good enough for me!

The big day out

I've travelled this weary world of ours by land, and air, and sea,
And I think that I've seen about everything that's ever
   appealed to me –
Exotic sights, like the Northern Lights, or the jungles of Brazil,
Or the Taj Mahal by moonlight – and I marvel at them still.

Yet, wherever I have wandered, or no matter where I've been,
And in spite of all the things I've done, or all the sights I've seen,
I swear that there is nothing that gave me such great joy
As when I went to Bangor on the steam-train, as a boy.

I remember the excitement, and the sheer exhilaration
As I clutched my pennies in my hand and went down to the station,
And the special smell of burning coal was magic in the air
To an innocent wee fellow who didn't have a care.

Then, when the train got started, and chugged along the track,
I'd open up the window, my face all sooty black,
And I'd look up to the engine, to try to see it flame –
And I'd see a hundred little boys doing just the same.

I remember, when I got there, the skies were blue and bright,
The sun was always shining, the temperature just right,
And I'd head at once for Pickie, and splash about the pool
With my shoulders getting sun-tanned, and the water nice and cool.

And when I'd finished swimming, I'd head down to the shore
And I'd hunt the pools for shrimps and crabs, and catch them
   by the score;
After that, I'd go and buy a 'slider' or a 'poke'
(For in those days we hadn't heard of hamburgers or Coke!).

I'd try to skim a stone or two on every seventh wave.
And at last I'd head for Barry's, a real Aladdin's cave,
And there I'd look about me, my wee mouth open wide
In wonder and amazement at everything I spied.

I'd feed my pennies in the slots, and I would stand and stare
At the Laughing Man, the Gypsy, the old Electric Chair;
I'd even have a gamble, for I would have a go
To try to make my fortune, with three pears in a row. . .

And I'd go and ride the bumpers, while the sparks flew overhead,
But all the time I watched the clock with ever-mounting dread,
And my poor wee heart was heavy, and filled with desolation
When I had to dash from Barry's up to Bangor railway station.

If it happened that I'd tuppence left (and if the train was late),
I'd go and punch my name out on an aluminium plate;
I'd make the odd mistake or two, and the end result looked queer,
But at least I'd gone and got myself a Bangor souvenir!

Well, that was many years ago, my childhood's long since gone,
And now my hair is turning grey, and I am getting on,
But still I've got a yearning to go there once again,
So excuse me, now – I'm heading off . . . to catch the Bangor train!

The garden

Would you look at my dahlias, they're failures,
   and the greenfly has flummoxed my phlox;
My sunflowers stoop, my delphiniums droop,
   and something has savaged my stocks;
My willow tree's wilted and terribly tilted,
   I've made a right ass of my asters,
And though it seems crazy, even my daisies
   turn out to be downright disasters.

My anenomes have their own enemies,
   my begonias are so woe-begone;

There's ants in my poor anthirrhinums,
    and masses of moss in my lawn;
My sweet peas are sour, my lobelias won't flower,
    my cornflowers suffer from bunions
And my radishes rot, my rose has black spot –
    and my sage bushes don't know their onions!

I tried some chrysants., but they're terrible plants,
    I can't seem to grow them at all;
My artichoke's croaked (by chickenweed choked),
    and my wallflower's gone to the wall;
My peas haven't flowered, for they've all been devoured
    by some insect that fancies their taste,
And some little hallions have ruined my scallions –
    the whole thing's a terrible waste. . .

It's really too bad to see just how sad
    are the hearts of my poor gladioli;
My thyme is too tardy, and not very hardy,
    and my Honesty looks most unholy;
My runner bean's walked, and my broad beans have baulked,
    my cucumber has lost all its cool,
And my marrow's no bone, and I grumble and groan
    at the hundreds of weeds I've to pull.

My lupin's in loops, the leaves curled in hoops,
    my nasturtium's nasty to view;
My savoys have all sagged, and my leeks all need lagged,
    and my daffodils don't seem to do;
My marigold's dead, for it's more mari-lead;
    as a flower it hadn't much mettle,
And my blackcurrant's bare . . . and I'm going to swear,
    for I've gone and been stung by a nettle.

My beetroot are beaten, won't ever be eaten,
    my apples would give you the pip;
My Love-in-a-Mist will never be kissed,
    my tulips all give me the slip;
The whole thing's a mess, and the answer, I guess,
    is to know I'm completely defeated,
And to buy some cement – for my urgent intent
    is to have the whole shambles concreted!

The space race

Now, the people of the village of Ballymagheroo
Decided it was time to show the world what they could do,
And so they had a meeting in the little village hall
To decide upon a project that would help them, one and all.
Of course, the credit for it all belonged to John Magee,
And they seized on his suggestion with great alacrity.
The excitement was contagious, and the dissidents were few.
The day they joined the Space Race in Ballymagheroo.

They formed a grand committee, with the vicar in the chair,
And the membership consisted of just everybody there –
They chose old Willie Wilson for his technical ability
(Although he wasn't noted for particular agility!)
Well, they built themselves a rocket out of fourteen rusty bins,
And used a set of combine blades as stabiliser fins –
The engine was a problem, and they hunted near and far,
Till Mickey Mack presented them with his old Morris car. . .

Now, fuel was the snag, of course, for petrol's very well,
But you won't get very far in space on extra-mileage Shell,
But at last they found the answer – sure, the rocket would go fine
If the doctor's wife just filled it with her elderberry wine!
Another question then arose – just exactly who
Would volunteer as astronaut for Ballymagheroo?
But, enthusiastic though they were, 'twas really very queer
That in all the place, they couldn't find a single volunteer!

Although it wasn't quite the perfect way that they had planned,
They decided they'd no option but to send it off, unmanned!
With a Japanese transistor (which they chose, 'cause it was light),
And Joey Murphy's football, they made a satellite.
At last, the launching day arrived, the skies were clear and blue –
You'd swear the whole of Ireland came to Ballymagheroo!
There were hundreds of reporters, and the Television News,
Who watched as Widow Hanley took a match, and lit the fuse.

Such a rousing cheer went up, and what a mighty roar
As higher, higher into space that rocketship did soar!
Every eye was straining as it disappeared from view –
They'd really joined the Space Race in Ballymagheroo!
Now, if you've got a wireless that can pick up satellites,
You'll hear a most peculiar sound, if you listen in these nights,
For if, among the signals, there's one that goes 'Hic! Hic!'
You'll know that elderberry wine has gone and done the trick!

The wee blue beg

They say that progress must be made,
    a point, I'm sure, that true;
Old orders fade and pass away,
    to make room for the new –
But yesterday I met a man
    who thought the whole thing wrong,
And my heart was filled with sorrow,
    as I listened to his song. . .

'They've taken the wee blue beg away,
    the wee beg's gone for good,
'Without so much as a by-your-leave
    – I think they were bloomin' rude!
'They never asked no one's opinion,
    they just weren't playin' the game,
'For without thon wee blue beg of salt,
    me crisps don't taste the same!

'I mind how me fingers trembled,
    and me pulse thrilled to the chase
'As I hunted for thon wee beg of salt
    to find its hiding-place,
'And I mind thon fateful evenin',
    when me heartbeats nearly halted
'When I opened me beg of tatie crisps. . .
    to find they were ready-salted!

'What right had they to deprive me?
    They're just a bunch of dictators!
'They've taken away the power I had
    over me crisped potatoes!
'How can I ever enjoy them again,
    for what chance have I got
'To make me own decision
    as to salt me crisps or not?

'No matter wherever ye look, there's signs
    that your freedom is taken away –
'NO LEFT TURN! NO ENTRY!
    and SMOKING FORBIDDEN!, they say;
'They even do it at traffic lights,
    GO! GET READY! and HALT!
'And now they won't even allow ye
    to sprinkle your crisps with salt!

'There's a subtle, delicate balance, y'see,
    between the crisps and the salt,
'And now I can never strike it
    – and it's all their blinkin' fault!
'I've got no say in the matter now,
    I can't control the flavour,
'For without thon beg (if I can quote),
    the salt hath lost its savour!

'The wee blue beg has vanished
    – may thunder and lightnin' strike them!
'Why must they salt my crisps for me
    – they don't know how I like them!
'I reckon it's just contrariness,
    – or so it seems to me,
'For I'm sure they've plenty of wee blue begs
    down there in Tandragee!

'I can manage without me pint of beer,
    I can do without a feg,
'But in my crisps, I sorely miss
    the salt in the wee blue beg –
'So I'm going to start a movement,
    and me efforts will never slack. . .
'Till they yield to the will of the masses. . .
    and put thon wee beg back!'

The crime

They were packed to the walls in O'Hooligan's bar
And were having themselves quite a night,
And the porter was creamy, and blacker than tar,
And divil the woman in sight;
The lads let their hair down, as men always do
When they cannot be seen by the wife,
Aided along by a whiskey or two
To add a wee spice to their life.

Now, Johnny the barman was working flat out,
The sweat pouring down from his brow,
Dispensing the half 'uns and drawing the stout
As only an expert knows how,
When, all of a sudden, the door opened wide
And a silence fell down on the room
As Constable Kelly came plodding inside,
His face a grim warning of doom.

'I've reason to think there's a crime taking place,
'And I'm here, 'cause I'm looking for clues –
'It's a terrible business, an awful disgrace,
'For someone has doctored the booze!
'I'm reliably told that the whiskey you're drinkin'
'Has been mixed with the ould mountain dew –
'It's a divilish trick to be playin', I'm thinkin',
'On fine, dacent people like you!

'Now, Johnny', he said to the barman, 'Look here,
'I'm not sayin' that you are to blame,
'And I'd like to believe, son, that you're in the clear,
'And you'll help me to keep your good name?'
'I will, Mr Kelly, I will!' John replied,
'You will find that my whiskey is pure,
'For the law must be kept, and I'm on your side –
'My conscience is clear, that's for sure!'

'Well, I'll need to take samples', the Constable said,
'Say, a bottle of each single brand –
'Sure, we can't have this thing hangin' over your head,
'And you're lucky that I understand.
'Now, suspicion like this could be bad for your trade,
'And you'd really have reason to grouse
'If the rest of the boys should find out, I'm afraid. . .
'So I'll test them myself, in the house. . .'

Well, the constable left (with the bottles, to test),
And wee Doyle, he got up to his feet:
'Three cheers for oul' Kelly; he's one of the best!
'Sure, discretion like that can't be beat!'
'Discretion, me barney!' Johnny said, with a scowl,
'That divil's oul' heart is pure black,
'For he comes that oul' tale all the time – on me sowl
'At the same time next month, he'll be back!'

Feeling fragile

I'm feelin' sort of fragile, and far from hale and hearty –
I must have had a smashin' time at Willie Wilson's party!
I can't mind much about it, but I must have had a ball,
For the fact is, at the moment, I don't feel good at all!

I've a sneakin' recollection of seein' Jinny Jones,
And I've got a sinkin' feelin' right down inside my bones
That I wasn't quite as sensible as might have been supposed
For, though I just can't stand her . . . I've a feelin' I proposed!

The trouble is, I can't think straight, for I had a right old sup,
And, boys, I'm awful worried that she went and took me up –
I just can't mind her answer, and I don't know what to do,
But one thing's sure and certain – I'm in a fair old stew. . .

I know I ought to phone her, but I'd get an awful fright
If I discovered what I'm fearing turns out to be right!
I cannot even write to her, for then, without a doubt,
If she had it down on paper, I could never wriggle out!

Didn't I? Or did I? The answer's got me vexed;
Small wonder that I'm lookin' green, and feelin' fierce perplexed!
Have I gone and stuck my silly head inside the bridal halter?
Are my days of freedom numbered? Am I headed for the altar?

What did Jinny answer me, all those hours ago?
Oh, boys, I'd be delighted if I thought that she'd said 'No!'
Just think, a drop of porter has led to my undoin',
And a glass or two of whiskey has brought me near to ruin. . .

Here, wait a minute – there's the phone! 'Hello? . . . Yes, this is me.
'Oh . . . Jinny . . . it's yourself . . . well, no . . . I'm not exactly
      free. . .'
'You want to ask a question? Well . . . all right . . . go ahead. . .'
'Here, wait a minute, Jinny – what was that you said. . .?'
'You say you're feelin' fierce ashamed at what you did last night?'
'You had a drop too much to drink, and passed out like a light?'
'You cannot mind the things you said? And now you want to
      know. . .?'
'I'm sorry – I've forgotten, too . . . So, Jinny, cheerio!'

The Angel of Sandy Row

One Saturday night, I'd been having a jar
And was walking back home from a Sandy Row bar;
I'd had far too many, it wasn't no joke,
So I turned up an entry as I felt I could boke. . .
When I lifted my head, I felt even more sicker,
And I swore, there and then, that I'd give up the liquor,
For, standin' before me, all shiny and bright,
Was a figure that gave me one helluva fright!
He'd great flowin' robes that came down till his ankle –
The likes of thon never was seen up the Shankill!
Sez he, 'I'm an angel!' Sez I, 'Ye're a *what?*'
Sez he, 'I'm an angel!' Sez I, 'That ye're not,
'For, if ye're really an angel, then where are yer wings,
'And why aren't ye pluckin' yer heavenly strings,
'And surely ye've got better places till go
'Than standin' up entries in oul' Sandy Row?'
Sez he, 'Willie, dear, I'm here in disguise,
'For I'm one of the Oul' Man's heavenly spies –
'Though up there, they think I'm a bit of a laugh,
'For me number is double-oh-six and a half!
'He's sent me till Ulster for till look at the scene
'And find out the difference 'twixt Orange and Green,
'For we've heard nasty rumours that Satan is grinnin',
'And that evil and badness in Ulster are winnin'!'
Sez I, 'Mister, dear, it's the truth that ye're speakin',
'For them Fenians all over the Province are sneakin' –
'They're gettin' in everywhere, man, but they're tricky;
'Ye could never be up till the games of a Mickey!'
Well, the angel, he looked at me hard, for a while,
Then he lifted his head, and he gave a wee smile –
It was like he was laughin' at some private joke,
And a feelin' of anger in me was awoke. . .
So, sez I, 'Listen, Mac – are ye Fenian or Prod?'
Sez he, 'Willie, dear, I'm the same as my God,
'And he doesn't care if ye're black or ye're white,
'If ye're Orange or Green, if ye're left or ye're right,

'If your family's all Prods, or Fenians, or Yids,
'For everyone here is one of His kids. . .'
Now, ye'll agree that a statement like that was a shocker;
It was clear as a bell he was clean aff his rocker,
And he surely knew nothin' at all about God
If he thought that a Mick was as good as a Prod!
Was he one of them students having a jest?
I decided till put the idea till the test,
So sez I, 'Tell us this, have ye heard of King Billy?
'Or even the Sash, or the fair Orange lily?
'D'ye know of the Blues, or of brave Derry's walls?
'Did ye know that Oul' Nick has a house up the Falls?'
Well, he just shook his head, and leaned back on the wall.
Sez I, 'D'ye not know yer Bible at all?'
Now, I go to church like every Prod should,
And decided to do the poor fella some good,
And I said, 'Tell ye what, I'm takin' ye home,
'And, afore ye go back, ye'll know all about Rome –
'When ye're up there in Heaven, ye'll have lots new till tell. . .
'Like, for instance, the divil speaks Gaelic in Hell!'
Well, in no time at all, we were back at my house,
And there, at the dure, was Big Jinny, my spouse,
And the luk on her bake made me wake at the knees,
So, quick as a flash, sez I, 'Jinny, please,
'I want ye till meet a good buddy of mine –
'I don't know his name, but his number'll do fine;
'He's one of them spies, like thon double-oh-seven,
'And, belave it or not, his headquarters is Heaven!
'He's come for his supper, so get out the pan,
'And act like ye married a dacent wee man!'
Well, her gub was a picture, but give her her due,
She stuck out her hand, and said, 'How d'ye do?
'From Heaven till Belfast is many's a mile,
'So now that ye're here, ye must stop for a while!'
One thing about Jinny, she knows how till bake,
And there, on the table, she put ANGEL cake!
And yer man was that pleased, ye could tell by his face,
That he said, 'Here, I'm glad I came down till this place!'
Well, after the tay, we sat down for a chat

And we talked about this, and we talked about that,
And I tould him the way that things were in Belfast,
And how all us Prods would fight till the last
And keep Ulster free from Fenian blood,
The way that our forefathers said that we shud,
And I tould him about my own LOL,
And I showed him me sash (and I wore it, as well),
And then I brought out me wee Orange flute
And decided till give it a bit of a toot. . .
I played him 'The Sash', and I played 'Dolly's Brae',
And, sez he, 'Willie, man, ye fairly can play –
'But lend us yer flute, and I'll give ye an air
'That's just a bit different from them ye played there!'
So I gave him the flute, and he started till play. . .
Lord, I'll never forget thon till my dyin' day,
For the notes that he played made us sit there, quite still;
They rose up in the air, the whole house for till fill;
They were soft. . . they were sweet. . . they brought tears till
    me eyes. . .
And I suddenly felt. . . so old. . . and so wise. . .
Then a funny thing happened, and I'll tell ye no lie –
Yer man touched me arm. . . and I started till *fly!*
With him at me side, I rose up in the air,
And out of the house, over Shaftesbury Square;
I was that bloomin' scared that I started till shiver,
And me arms and me legs were all of a-quiver
As the two of us kept floatin' on through the night,
Passin' the oul' City Hall on the right,
And there was the shipyard, the Dufferin Dock,
The Liverpool boat, and the oul' Albert Clock,
And there were the people, the girls and the boys,
And the lights of the city, the smells, and the noise,
The hooting of horns, and also, of course,
The police and the army were down there, in force –
Then all of a sudden, we began till fly faster. . .
Ach, meetin' yer man was a downright disaster!
We soared up the Falls, towards Andersonstown,
And that's where we stopped, and I had a look down;
The rooves of the houses were sort of transparent –

43

The reason, to me, was not too apparent;
There was one wee house I especially spied –
I could see right intil the bedroom inside;
You could tell at a glance where their loyalties lay,
For the Pope on the wall gave the whole game away!
And there was a man, on a wee wicker chair,
Lukkin' around with a sad, hopeless stare,
And a woman was there, at the fut of the bed. . .
When I lukked further up, me heart turned till lead;
When I saw what was there, I couldn't help cryin',
For there, on the bed, a wee child was lyin' –
And the funny thing was, when I saw it was sick,
It just didn't matter that it was a Mick. . .
The Fenians might breed families of nine,
But the wee child aisy cud be one of mine,
And its da cud aisy have been me own brother. . .
Ach, the Prods and the Micks were just like each other!
Now, whether or not 'twas because of the drink,
For the first time in ages, I started till think,
And I found I was tellin' meself till act wise,
And till luk all around me, and open me eyes. . .
Now, all of the time I was watchin' that room,
Yer man, on the flute, was still playin' that tune;
He handled the instrument just like a master. . .
Then all of a sudden, the tempo got faster
And we started till move away from Belfast,
And away from the present, and back till the past. . .
That music, it brought me right back till me youth,
To the first girl I'd loved, my darlin' wee Ruth;
I cud see her again, her eyes, and her smile –
I cud see us again, at the wee country stile –
And I minded the way that our families turned odd,
For she was a Mick . . . and I was a Prod. . .
I saw it again, the night Ruthie died,
And the way that her family had kept me outside. . .
I remembered all this, and I felt so . . . so sad,
For my folks turned out to be just as bad;
They tould me till marry intil me own,
Instead of a girl whose allegiance was Rome,

And, rememberin' this, I knew very well
There were Prods as well as Mickies in Hell!
And I minded, as well, that God sent His Son
For till say, 'Love yer Neighbour' – and He meant every one –
And, while I remembered, the music played on.
Then it stopped. I lukked up. The angel was gone. . .
Well, the next thing I knew, I woke up in bed
With a mouth like a sewer, and a bomb in me head,
And Jinny was lyin' there, tonguin' and screamin' –
Everythin' normal! I must have been dreamin'!
But it surely was one helluva drame,
For, from that day till this, I've not been the same,
For the music I heard lingers on in me mind,
And I swear that I'll never again be so blind –
Till the day that I die, I'll trate all men the same,
Even the ones with a Catholic name!
And, if God thinks I'm worth it, He'll take me to Heaven,
And make me a spy – maybe double-oh-seven?
And maybe, some day, if ye're up Sandy Row,
And up an oul' entry ye might have till go,
Who knows? Ye might see me, in a shiny white suit,
And there, in me hand, me wee Orange flute;
And, if ye ask me, real nice, I'll play ye that tune. . .
But now, I'm away. . . sure, I'll see ye. . . real soon. . .

Dear Ulster

Dear Ulster, where the dullis grows
And jokes need careful thinkin' –
Where a man can thump you on the nose,
Then ask you what you're drinkin'. . .

Dear Ulster, of the tatie bread
And mugs of steamin' tay,
Where men wear dunchers on their head
To keep the birds at bay. . .

Dear Ulster, where you meet new friends
That you can get real thick with –
Though, naturally, it all depends
Upon what foot you kick with. . .

Dear Ulster, where the colours glow
On every single human –
You'll see them everywhere you go,
The 'Orange', 'Green' or 'Blue' man. . .

Dear Ulster, of the open hearts,
And kindness that is rare,
For, if you hail from foreign parts,
You're welcome everywhere. . .

Dear Ulster, where the pubs all close
Too early every night,
Where black and creamy porter flows,
And wit is sharp and bright. . .

Dear Ulster, where traditions reign
And Yesterday is king,
Where Tomorrow and Today remain
A secondary thing. . .

Dear Ulster, stubborn as can be,
Its people dour and proud,
Who speak their minds quite fearlessly
And think their thoughts aloud. . .

Dear Ulster, fairest of the fair,
But a paradox, that's true –
In all the whole, wide world, I swear
There's nowhere quite like you!